ALSO BY MARCK L. BEGGS

POETRY
Catastrophic Chords (2008)
Libido Café (2004)
Godworm (1995)

EDITOR
*Poets of the Roundtable of Arkansas
80th Anniversary Anthology* (2013)

Blind Verse
Marck L. Beggs

salmonpoetry

Published in 2015 by
Salmon Poetry
Cliffs of Moher, County Clare, Ireland
Website: www.salmonpoetry.com
Email: info@salmonpoetry.com

Copyright © Marck L. Beggs, 2015

ISBN 978-1-910669-07-5

All rights reserved. No part of this publication may be reproduced or transmitted in any form or by any means, electronic or mechanical, including photography, recording, or any information storage or retrieval system, without permission in writing from the publisher. The book is sold subject to the condition that it shall not, by way of trade or otherwise, be lent, resold or otherwise circulated without the publisher's prior consent in any form of binding or cover other than that in which it is published and without a similar condition, including this condition, being imposed on the subsequent purchaser.

COVER ARTWORK: : *El Toro* by Amy Kohut
COVER DESIGN & TYPESETTING: *Siobhán Hutson*
Printed in Ireland by Sprint Print

Acknowledgments

Thank you to the editors of the following journals for originally publishing these poems:

Clade Song: "Blind Verse," "God & Dog"
Common Ground Review: "Pisces" and "Arkansas at Dusk"
Excelsior Review: "Troy" and "The Eros"
Foliate Oak: "Feline 101"
Ghoti: "Slinky"
Toad Suck Review: "Inanna Responds," and "The Predator's Mistress"

Thank you to Henderson State University for an Ellis College Research Grant that allowed me to travel to Iceland, Ireland, and Scotland to research and complete many of these poems.

Thank you Jessie and Siobhán at Salmon Poetry for your patience and kindness.

Thank you to the Tupelo Press's *30/30 Project* which challenged me to write a new poem every single day for a month. It was exhausting and exhilarating at once. Most of all, it got me back on track right when I needed it.

Thanks to all my friends and family members who accept that I am a poet before all the other things that I am (or have to be). And thanks most of all to my wife, Carly, who has made my life better than I thought it could be, and who has helped create an atmosphere where I can write.

Finally, thank you to my parents, Conrad and Audrey Beggs, who passed before they could read all of this. I would be nothing without their love and support.

Contents

Travelogue

Pisces	11
Pussy Riot Speaks to Amerika	12
Cat on a Cold Tin Roof	13
The Phallological Museum in Reykjavik	14
Gauksmýri	15
Þorgeir's Bull	16
Char	17
The Cynic's Calendar	18
Mondæg Sestina Variation	19
Tiwesdæg Pantoum	21
Wonesdæg Sonnet	22
þunresdæg	23
Friġedæġ	24
Sæternesdæg	25
Sunnandæg	26
Inanna Responds	27
Troy	29
The Predator's Mistress	30
The Evil Sister	31
Morals	32

Lyrics and Narratives

Wraith	35
Blind Verse	36
Blind Verse 2	37
Carly Walking	38
Ireland	39
The Irish Poet	40

Arkansas at Dusk	41
Tucson	42
Alaska	43
Bully Poem	44
Sex Ed	45
The Eros	46
My My My My Corolla	48
Vinyl	49
Duck Man	50
Living Room Ghazal	51
Feline 101	52
Slinky	54
God & Dog	55
Dead Bird	56

Travelogue

Pisces

My rightful name is held underwater
and I was born into a month of massacres:
Boston, My-lei, the Alamo. I remember nothing
beyond the algae stench of youth.
The gods were cruel then as now:
casting my stars in the bleakest corner
of the universe, cursing me awake with dreams
bobbing like serpents between black waves.

Pussy Riot Speaks to Amerika
dedicated to the Arkansas Democrat-Gazette

Mr. Putin will make you love your country
the same way you came to adore the man
who walked up from behind, choked a hood
over your head, and locked you in a dark
basement that smelled of fear and piss.
Every breath belonged to him, every
minute was his to interrupt or ignore,
every sip of water suckled from his teat of kindness.

Your own country is confused by all of this.
Your free press will publish photographs
of women viciously whipped by a Cossack,
yet determine our name too obscene to print.
Are words truly less than a picture in America?
Does this onslaught of feline vaginas and art offend
your inky wretches so much that they would deny us
before the cock has begun to crow?

We are not invisible, Amerika, and
we are not unnamed. When words become
more delicate then crushed flesh, your own name
becomes the berserk boot heel of history.

Cat on a Cold Tin Roof

If you leave open a window
or a sliding porch door, the cats
of Reykjavik will slink
into your dreams, stretch out
on your copy of *Grapevine*,
and shed elven locks
to lurk among your private clothing.

At any moment, you might stroll along
a side alley off Laugavegur
and look up, suddenly, into the algae stare
of a tabby on a fir-tinted roof contemplating
the crest of your skull. It will stop you
dead in your tracks, much like
your first Sunday morning in the city,

among the street sweepers,
Norwegian forest cats, calicos, and spooks
flitting in and out of the alleys
as the final dregs of human wildlife
pour out from six a.m. liquid doors
to wind their way toward somewhere familiar, avoiding
the Lutheran church, a singular mountain

upon a hill, ringing them home.
Except that home for the youth
of Iceland is found in pale light,
translucent as skin. If only the bells
tolled for the cats: they would climb the tower
to spread such unperceivable gospels.

The Phallological Museum in Reykjavik

If sadness were a sheath of mist
enshrouding the Matterhorn to its base,
one might wail into the waning Icelandic night
for the maritime martyrs who inhabit this hall.

Once, the Northern oceans were crowded
with penes the size of small boats.
Now they cringe like born-again hobos
in massive tubes of formaldehyde.

The once proud sperm whale reduced
to driftwood, the dolphin exposed
for its diminutiveness. Nor are the tundra
dwellers safe from this carnal carnival.

That the reindeer's member shines red
as Rudolph's nose is no consolation
for its detachment at the edge
of a curator's manful blade.

Gauksmýri

On the horse farm they serve horse
to eat, ride, or pet. Snug in a lonely valley
where Vikings must have dreamed
under low clouds before opting
to give up on the sea, the gods
opened their eyes to such barren beauty.
Clearly, the horses know. From beneath
their wind-tossed, voguish manes,
they watch to see if you are worth the effort.

The Icelandic horse is its own legend.
Among the ancients, white horses were slaughtered
in the name of fertility. Odin's Sleipnir
boasted eight legs and was borne of Loki,
who transformed himself into a mare, luring
the seed of Svaðilfari. Loki: mother of a horse,
father of a wolf. Loki the salmon,
Loki the fog. His suffering roused earthquakes,
his insults sprayed infective lunacy.

It was not Loki's horse-child who finally
killed Odin, but his wolf. For any man
may devour a horse and live. But Fenrir
would ingest the gods themselves—hand or whole—
to drink the mead of poetry.

Þorgeir's Bull

In the cool hour of dark mist, what
Portuguese fishermen term *madrugada*,
I weave through your village, a ribbon of fog.
You will recognize me in a flash
of clarity: the skeleton horse
with my own split skin flapping from my haunches,
an unbelievable flag to warn
of nothing that you may undo.
Within my ribs, you might perceive
my alter-selves: skogkatt, raven, Lagarfljót worm,
wolf-eel, wolfhound, pika, pauper, or miasma.

My fathers trained me to asphyxiate the brains
of women they could not tame. To bury them
within their own souls, to spirit them
under rocks where not even the huldufólk
could save them from the wrath of jealous men.

Char

You stare at musty, foreign
wallpaper for hours, convinced
it threatens you. Your brow furrows
like the northwestern fjords on the blank map
of a face you no longer recognize.
Narcissus has abandoned you in the wake
of New Age trolls sensitive as lambs
regarding their physical appearance,
yet haughty under the groan of the moon.
You thought you had never listened before
to moonlight, but why not? For years
you preached the gospel of alternative breathing,
and how did that work out? Not so well
for the Arctic Char drying
on your plate. You met him underwater
in a sea-pond bluer than a Coltrane flat-note.
He asked you for guidance, and you
suggested an intimate dinner
near the harbor. Hours later, as he gurgled
through your intestines, you watched out
over a sunlit Keflavik bay at midnight
humming a tune approximating jazz
or blues or even the sonorous spray
of the sea itself. The fish taught you
something, but you passed out in a freezing lounge chair
before the sageness could take its bait.

The Cynic's Calendar

The April fool may be cruel,
but the August Nazi drops
us to our knees, sweltering,
mosquito-bitten, begging for water.

July is an idiot blowing up the landscape,
celebrating war. December and January
meet in a violent kiss of anarchy,
each dismissing the other at midnight.

The November fascist pretends
to belong to two seasons, then
opens the door to carnage, saturating
the forests with the blood of turkeys and deer.

February settles for anything thrown
in its short path: a celebration of women,
African Americans, presidents, and Civil War traitors.
As if history itself passed in a fragment.

May brings daffodils smothered by October,
so much yellow drained to burnt orange.
June and September swing in the wind
like a broken screen on a rusty door-hinge.

And here is how it appears through the eyes
of March: Earth's slow-bus passage of time,
the retarded progress of humankind
slobbering its mortal way to the sublime.

Mōndæg Sestina Variation

With the day of the moon
comes the usual lunacy:
a child fair of face,
another stag slain by a goddess,
the masses plodding back to work,
the yellow aura of cancer and suicide.
It is a day to avoid.

There is much in life to avoid.
One should never punk a goddess,
or prepare voodoo dolls at work.
One should never commit suicide
without a well-designed death face.
One should never confuse the moon
with cheese unless one has slipped into lunacy.

There are specific signs to support lunacy.
For instance, you wake up at work
and suddenly your inner goddess
is sad and plans her suicide.
This can easily be avoided.
Just stare into a mirror until your face
swells up like the moon.

When you begin to resemble the moon,
you will remember that suicide
is illegal, and you never break the law. A goddess
doesn't have to cheat. She can drive a man to lunacy
through the sheer will of her face.
Which is another thing to avoid:
the Medusa in the cubicle at work.

Trust me. I know how this all works.
After all, I am a failure at suicide,
yet I have driven many a woman to lunacy,

something I probably should have avoided.
But now I have a woman who stares at the moon
and it stares back into her face.
She is a moonful goddess.

And she has the moods of a goddess.
So I have to look her in the face
and explain that, in the Netherlands, the moon
is a peculiar shade of lunacy.
That's just how the world works.
Otherwise, it could all be avoided,
and no one would sink into suicide.

Besides, isn't it a bit cliché to wind up a suicide?
How many bridges can you leap from in the light of the moon?
Will your death note blame it on lunacy?
Will you curse the lunar goddess
behind the yellow cubicle at work?
Is it her fault that you have a face
that, to be polite, you might want to avoid?

Look. It's just Monday. Avoid going to work,
don't think about the goddess or suicide.
Stay up late and face the lunacy of the moon.

Tiwesdæg Pantoum

For the honor of the day
I allowed the wolf to bite off my hand
One day, he will swallow the All-father
and I will die in the teeth of dogs.

I allowed the wolf to bite off my hand,
but it was never offered. The creature was bound.
I will die in the teeth of dogs,
but without the weapon of my hand.

It was never offered. The creature was bound
in miraculous ribbons forged with six elements.
Without the weapon of my hand,
how could I wield a sword?

The miraculous elements were forged with six elements
of a metaphorical nature, now gone from this world.
How shall I wield a sword
for the honor of this day?

Wōnesdæg Sonnet

Today, the sun shines gray. The woeful child
fashions ash to her forehead to begin
another month of penance. Another
week of gloom. Another day to rescind.

Odin knows who will be born tomorrow
and it fills his brain with a leaking dread,
to know a son beyond his own powers,
to understand his own fate, his own death.

To be devoured by Fenrir, to die
in the belly of a wolf is to pass
from this world in a flash of shit, only
to hope a son will bring an end to this.

The woeful lives of gods are fraught with pain.
We humans sacrifice, but to what gain?

Þunresdæg
for Farley (2000-2014)

Forget the myths for a day, even
if they belong to Thor. Today
belongs to Farley, named
after the great Canadian defender of wolves,
not the comedian. Today, Farley is going to die
and I will bury him in a watery hole.

I was born on a Thursday, so I figure
that I own it as much as anyone.
When I first brought him home,
the lake was solid ice. Farley slid
all over the surface, but on land
he ran circles around everything:
tractors, four-wheelers, even deer.

Then his legs broke. Surgeries,
tumors, deafness, confusion.
Farley limped through his final years
like any athlete too great to retire.
He was the Mohammad Ali of mutts.
He stamped this world with his face,
and limped off among the greats.

Frīgedæġ

Frigga knows your future,
but she's not telling. Perhaps
it is a good day to plant potatoes,
or a bad day to set sail. Either way,
you'll have to get through this by yourself.

Frigga will spend the day spinning clouds
or assisting midwives. You will take
a nap and miss the entire weekend.
Frigga knew this and fed you dreams
of your husband departing to far lands
while his brothers divided your time.

But even Frigga mistook Loki
for a woman and fed him
the wrong secret. Loki handed a shaft
of mistletoe to a blind man
who flung it like a butterfly into Baldr's heart.

Sæternesdæg

Clearly, birds understand nothing
about the Jewish Sabbath.
The red hawk nestled in the gum tree
will eat anything it can carry away in its talons.

My cat should be more nervous about this,
but she is too busy ridding the world
of lizard tails. What is kosher to one species
is heretical, or at least disgusting, to another.

If, in the afterlife, lizards gather
around in judgment of Po-Poe, she
will have much to explain. She could argue
science: they all lived long and prosperous

lives without their tails. Or she could argue
emotion and addiction. She could recite
the story of my parents' dog,
a toad sucker and fermented apple junkie.

After days of sucking, he would spit
the dried-out husk of a toad onto the concrete,
stare at the water bucket, then
wander out to the orchard for his next buzz.

Melakhah was not on this dog's agenda.
But today it is on mine. For Shabatt
gives logic to my laziness for a day
when I am the world's most orthodox atheist.

Sunnandæg

Eventually, 4/20 and Easter
were destined to meet in a smokefest
of aura and brightly colored eggs.
Who is to say which is the better tradition?

I'll claim both. The man from Galilee
can bring the wine and fish; the Rastafarian
can bring mojo and hemp. It will be
a great and mellow day. My sister

will plant for the bees, while I
tear down the nests of wasps and dirt-daubers.
There is no day of rest. Otherwise,
the stagnant shall inherit the earth.

Inanna Responds

Gilgamesh lies like a two-headed snake,
boasting how he turned me away,
carving his own story,
his slant, into the walls of Uruk
because no one else could tell it with such *dexterity*.

Gilgamesh's brain is slow as a crippled eunuch,
and could not interpret his own dreams.
If a brick falls from a temple—
sudden blunder of a drunken slave—
he bolts to his doting mother.

And no doubt she discovers a sign
to keep the small puddle of his mind
swirling. "A friend!" she exclaims.
Finally, a friend will come for the great king,
someone who can stomach his stench and manners.

Allow me a word regarding his social graces:
raping new brides was just the beginning.
After enough beer, he would deflower grooms,
gourds, goats, and anything else in the room.
Gilgamesh lived to seed the whole of the Earth.

He views the world as his vessel for the filling.
I came back from the underworld
while this weakling not only sent a harlot
to tame Enkidu, but could not even grasp
a mere flower to save his own people.

Yes, this is your great king: creating adventure
solely for the right to boast,
adventures of no relevance to his people,
except to keep him away from the women
and livestock. A great king like an axe to the skull.

Believe whom you will. I spent enough of my life
among the dead, and I know too well
the plight of rumor and the afterlife of gossip.
One day, I shall lure Gilgamesh to my lower bed
and hand him his own skin to wipe his tears.

Troy
for Helen

What any of us know about beauty
Could dance on the head of a pin
And follow the hallucination of death
And his three-headed mistress.

Yet you stand there
Wounded by memory. Bloody
As birth. Beautiful as raw sunlight
Splitting grey clouds.

The great lie of history
Is that we crave peace. We crave
Beauty at the brutal price of loss:
A man's life for a fair cheek,

The slaughter of oxen for a god's favor.
The salted wind pocketing a man's face
Across the ocean never blinds him
To the icon within his heart.

Beneath that golden helmet,
Your eyes are the sad, deep mirrors
In which we see our own terrible hearts.
We should have protected you. We should have

Held you back from the world.
But can any man prevent the sun?
For every arrow piercing a heel
Is a man contemplating a lost woman.

So how do I tell you any of this?
I feel you at night, remember your words.
I smell you down to the bones
And I would have you unlocked.

The Predator's Mistress

Shake out the crumpled tinfoil
of his sermon and snakes
caress your cheeks like linen
clutching a mother's clothesline,
billowing with lover's breath.

His prophecy is not of this world,
but for mine. Other women haggle
like fleas over worldly matters
once he has cut them loose
as the Chinese lock of his hair.

They believe laws transcend, but I
am his *protégée*. I sense
the various and sundry nuance
of his words, the rhetoric of my blood.
I live within, and my own husband is his mirror.

I bear false witness against his enemies.
I bear malice unto those who deny his love.
I bear warnings of fire and law.
I am his word pressed against your temple.
I am the black star behind the sun.

The Evil Sister

is filled with money.
Mercurial dimes clog her arteries
like river sludge. She is the darkest
corner of a vicious alley
off the Avenue of Rage.
She is the cult of lies and herpes.

When we were young, her fists
fit my body like grooved shingles.
Her eyes were bursts of madness.
She craved the company of spiders and moss.
She worshiped the science of pain.

The evil sister lost her way
within a man beaten down by dullness
and hubris. His brain a cracked rock of ego.
His life measured by the coin and the bruise.

Morals

Everything is normal in a fairy tale.

The daughters of incestuous fathers
must cloak themselves within miraculous armoires
or the skins of bears. And when she finds her way
to the prince, something about the bear
speaks out to him, touches his soul,
until he grows weak and sickly. So he has the beast
brought into his chambers to cook
and care for him as not even his own mother's soup
can bring warmth and hope to his parched heart.

Eventually, of course, the boy wants to kiss the bear,
and the mother approves. She harbors no inkling
of Freudian guilt, nor does she suspect
that the beast might be an illusion.
Simply a mother who desires a happy, healthy son.
So she stands aside, observing as the bear
boils up a kettle of leek & lentil soup.
She does not even gasp at the sight
of her son approaching a bear in an amorous way.

Fortunately, she is a lucky woman and the bear
turns out to be a beautiful young girl running from her past.
However, this was a risky move on the girl's part
because, after all, the prince was going for the bear.
Suppose the prince did not swing her way?
Suppose that, once you go bear,
you have no more thoughts for beautiful young girls?

Lyrics and Narratives

Wraith

When I dream of my parents,
they appear in the future,
as if memory had slipped
beneath the glacier of time.

Audrey peers out over the bay
toward Alameda and asks if I can see
the ghosts on the bridge. I can't, but
they make her smile. "You should look harder,"
she tells me. "One day you'll need them."
Her eyes are hazel again and clear.
The cataracts and foaminess evanesced.

Conrad is hanging feeders brimming
with black-oil sunflower seeds
for birds which have not yet arrived.
"When you no longer have birds to feed,"
he tells me, "your land is dead. And son,
I hope you never see that day."
But I already know it is coming.

Dad is tall and thin like in the photograph
where he is pulling a jack-o-lantern on a sled
in Alaska, waving. It was mom's favorite
and she insisted on it for his funeral
because he looked happy and he was waving
goodbye. Dashing in his uniform, he disappeared
in and out of our lives on Air Force missions.

I want this future: my mother the beautiful
officer's wife, my father the mysterious pilot.
I wish I had recognized it then, and that
it was all ahead of me. The clear horizon of my past.

Blind Verse

I was certain that blindness was a form
of darkness, a quick drop into the hole
or a cave where I led thirteen people—
blind as proverbial bats—down dark stairs.

We paused at the final turn, *a volta
of black light*, I declared. We would become
witnesses to a dark so pure, crickets
lived blind and translucent among the dust.

A dark so pure, I insisted, *that should
we remain here for a month, retinas
would die and we would spend our last days dark.*
I clicked off the lights and laughter erupted.

   *   *   *

Darling, forever I have been the fool.
Watching you lean into a book—gold light
flashing off your hair, a shadow halo
shifting along the wall—at least I know
there is a world of carved words between us.

Moreover, I know the scent of your hair
spread like leaves over a pillow is cause
for a night filled with unexpected dreams,
so rare in the empty space of my nights,
like a planet discovered through blind chance.

But you are more than dream, tiny darling—
standing up to faint, sitting down to pout—
if there were a single word to hold you,
it would stand forth clear as wind, and declare
itself so blind we missed it for the world.

Blind Verse 2

I need to read you in braille, in cool wind
on the shore of the lake. I want to smell
you with my tongue like a serpent winding
through the garden. When evening droops over
your shoulders like a shawl of negative
light, the horizon will glow lavender
and lift the shoreline to its lips. And then
we will hear the dark moaning through our skin.

The county dogs howl like snapping timbers
in the fire of another decade.
Wind-chimes play colorless chords for the deaf.
The tree line is silent, remembering
through the darkness the outline of your face—
which can rarely see itself—forged in grace.

Carly Walking

Our quarter-mile driveway serves
as her personal track, and she hikes it
for hours, Howard Stern perving her earbuds.
The path is full of adventure. For over a month,
she insists there is a monkey in a tree
near the main road. I walk down and,
indeed, hear a screeching up among
the treetops. But I cannot see anything,
and why would a monkey be on my tree farm
in Arkansas? Eventually, a neighbor
unravels the mystery: one tree has collapsed
against another, and they rub in the wind
like a violin out of tune. We are seriously disappointed.

Another time, she is nearly trampled by deer.
A dead snake won't scoot off the road.
Rabbits spring from nowhere.
Hawks circle above, squirrels jabber
and flit among the pine branches.

Through it all, Carly walks and walks
like a woman on her way to the end of time.

Ireland

Even the weeds smell ornamental,
short sniffs of lavender and liquor.
The pale sun moans behind old clouds,
wind-shifting between waltz and nostalgia.

Birds inhabit insane kings,
heroes play the roles of dogs,
and the crowned princess of the bog
lifts her head to the shovel's scrape and ping.

The Irish Poet

Kevin Higgins has the worst posture
of any poet in Irish history.
I suspect that if you pushed him
down a flight of stairs, his
lanky physique would respond
gracefully as a slinky, bouncing
down stair from stair to our collective
amusement and amazement. I suspect
aliens will want to study him one day.

The history of Irish posture is thick
with pain, like yoga in a gravel pit.
Ireland's greatest hero, Cú Chulainn,
had to prove himself by crouching like a dog
to pay back the death of an actual dog that he,
himself, slaughtered. Seamus Heaney tilted
like the Leaning Tower of Whiskey.
And Yeats dropped to his knees
to hear the whisper of a fairy.

In African folklore, a frog
swallows Cinderella and vomits her out,
but she is crooked, leaning to one side.
So he swallows her again until
he gets it right. But that original purge
is what explains the Irish Poet:
imperfect, tragic, and a little bent.

Arkansas at Dusk

For the pinprick of a moment
it is nearly beautiful:

    the oppressive heat slips off
    one's shoulders like silk.
    The fledgling sparrows have not yet
    fallen onto the unforgiving asphalt.
    The geese have settled among shadows
    and blue gills plop just over the lake's
    billowy surface to nab mosquitoes and dragonflies.

But in the dark, Nature will have her way.
The hungry beast sleeping
among the underbrush and thorns
watches out for her own, and even
when she goes silent from the rifle's repeat,
she will wait a lifetime, or less,
to rivet your eyes with dirt and wrap you in roots.

Tucson

From atop Mount Lemon, the city lights
boil the desert to a sludge of dark.
The higher air hums in static windstops,
fluttering like manes around blackened rocks.

The peyote settled, I would begin
my descent, stepping off a large boulder
which sprouted wings and flew to the ravens.
The dark bird within me sighed and whispered.

I ached for my mattress, cool on the roof,
the heat swelling up in the morning sun.
Tonight my bed would be leathery tough
and my dreams a practice for creation.

The rooftops of Tucson are littered with boys
alert under stars, mad ravens deployed.

Alaska

Among the wolves there is no past.
I am shoveling snow and they stare
at me like today's lunch.
It is 20 below zero: my breath
turns to clouds and my heart freezes.

They know I am alone.
They know a shovel will not save me.
They know they can run me down.
And they know, strangely, that I am not afraid.

Bully Poem

Today's poem is going to kick
your proverbial ass and show
no mercy. It's going to ram
a size-13 wingtip so far
up your sphincter that your breath
will smell like shoe polish.

This poem is going to steal
your lunch money, then hack
into your Facebook account
to replace your profile picture
with a pornographic image
involving unicorns and your sister.

This poem is going to collect
all your letters to the editor,
along with your teenage poems,
and self-publish them in a book
entitled, *An Idiot's Guide to the Universe.*
And then this poem is going to post
crass and disturbing reviews of the book
on Amazon.com. A dozen per day
for a year. Eventually, you will
receive a long missive from the entire
publishing industry insisting
that you emigrate both from the country
and from the English language. They will offer
a one-way, first class ticket to Tierra del Fuego.

Take the money and run. It's your only chance.
Otherwise, this poem is headed directly
to your home, where it will proceed
to break all your dishes and clog up your plumbing.
This poem will smoke camels in your bed
and forget to feed your cat. It will leave
behind a trail of mold that will require
a government agency to remove. This poem
takes no prisoners, and you are no exception.

Sex Ed

Why let a teacher talk to your kids about sex
when you can just take them out to the farm
to observe, first hand, how Nature
tackles this delicate subject?
Watch carefully as Herman the Muscovy
rapes each and every other waterfowl
on the surface of the lake,
male or female. Bring the binoculars
so you can truly appreciate his technique
as he mounts his intended, gently grasping
the back of the lover's neck with his beak,
and shoves his or her face under water
until the consummation is complete.

Now you can begin to explain to your offspring
how homosexuality is not natural, how Herman
is a special kind of drake, a Caligula,
if you will. Then you can explain Caligula
and spend the afternoon reciting the poems of Catullus.
Don't get too technical or hand the kids
any pamphlets written by a psychologist
of German descent. Keep it metaphorical
and awkward, as is the family tradition.
Eventually, the Internet will explain
it all to them in high definition.

The *Eros*

How a 350-ton ship
in the Merchant Marines
earned the name of this god
remains a mystery to me.

A crew of six—five seamen
and me, "college boy"— delivered
equipment and food to rigs
all over the Gulf of Mexico.

Captain Lou weighed nearly 300 pounds,
drank two fifths of Wild Turkey
per day, and sweated like
a frat boy in a maternity ward.

He once ran into a barge,
staring into the radar instead
of out the window. He once got lost,
directionally, in the Mississippi river.

But he also once saved my life.
Tied up against another ship, I thought
I could make the jump between, but
went down like a shot seagull.

Drunk as he was, Captain Lou
tossed down a rope and pulled
me up seconds before the ships
clanked together, heavy as iron whales.

That night, I sat out
on the dock playing harmonica
to a wild dolphin family
of exceptional musical taste.

They clucked and neighed at me
under a moon lording over the sea,
king of a million jelly fish
rising like alien globs.

Had I died that day,
I like to think the dolphins
would have garbed me in seaweed
for the slow float down.

My My My My Corolla

It was my first car, small
with a massive 8-ball stick shift.
Not exactly a chick magnet,
but it got us around.

Sometimes, chicks were actually involved,
but only because of John with his long hair.
Plus he could talk in front of girls,
and he understood their music.

I understood nothing at that age
beyond baseball, Anne Sexton,
and the Kinks. Anne was no help
whatsoever in trying to impress girls.

I would recite a line from *The Awful Rowing
Toward God*, and that would be the end
of a date. I should have quoted
Ray Davies: "I am an apeman."

I had trouble understanding friendships.
After we ate, they tossed trash
out my windows. I would stop, back up,
and ask them to bring the trash back in.

Suddenly, I was the jerk
among the idiots. I filled that Corolla
with multiple layers of trash, some
of whom could talk, some of which was tossed.

It finally died on the outskirts
of Mt. Pleasant, Texas. The engine block
cracked like a walnut. I called my dad
and sat for half a day smoking doobies

and fearing the worst. But dad
showed up in his Chrysler New Yorker, laughed
his ass off, sold off the Corolla for junk,
and drove me all the way home.

Vinyl

There I was, four years old,
and told to stay in the house.
But outside were my brother
and the one-eyed baby sitter,
fresh back from training,
with a scar and patch.
They were winging a copy
of *Surfin' Safari* back and forth
like a Frisbee. I couldn't take it,
bursting through the back door
like a dam break. It all happened
in slow motion: wind caught vinyl
and sent it to me. 120 grams
of *Surfin' Safari* lodged in my skull.

Duck Man

The old Russian wheels backwards
down a twenty-foot plank
from the opening of his doorless single-wide
to his duck cages, where two dozen
Pekins live on a six-inch, rock-hard carpet
of compressed shit. He rattles a stick to push them
toward the center. "You like eggs?"
I want to insert the tips of my fingers
into his fat eyes and poke their yokes.
The pen is three-feet high and I crawl
over this asphalt of shit for forty-five minutes
until I have wrangled up as many
as he is willing to sell. For the next month,
my knees are scarred with shit
burned in my skin. Peroxide becomes
a daily habit. I want to push the old Russian
into the pen and let him lie
among the stench of own making.
The duck man loves his ducks,
but such love is not worth the living.

Living Room Ghazal

The guitar in its stand is lovely but mute.
The guitar in my hand is a sorrowful lute.

Dogs sleep by the fire dreaming deeply as stones,
but soon they'll awaken to snorting and bruit.

A clock on my wall has ticked down to silence,
as if time has become increasingly moot.

The light through the window sways in a mad dance
to music from the lake, refrains of wild coots.

In tonight's sky, I will mark the red planet,
but for now I'll sit with this sorrowful lute.

Feline 101

Personality
One cat has an empty eye
socket, sees life from a left telescopic view,
astronomer charting half a sky.
Another runs with the dogs, fetches
mice like newspapers. A third sits,
Sphinx in the small sands of his box.

Weather
Poor dogs. From even the lowest clouds,
they break legs against the earth. They
roll over just in time to see that, for the cats, it's
just another branch. The dogs close their eyes
against the tips of claws pushing inward,
the grip of cats falling in the rain.

Martial Arts
We learn a stance, *neko ashi dachi*,
cat-stance. And more, that fingers strike first
for the eyes, rake down the face.
But this is all from a corner, hair rising
off our backs. Running being the honest choice.

Furniture
With a truly excellent feline collection, I never
have to rearrange a room; shifting complements
among the shelves, chairs, rugs,
they follow sunlight's sleepy gaze from window
to window.

In January, cats mat an abstract
quilt, something
to interpret in dreams.
Slumber is ambition. Humans,

those futuristic pillows.
> *Anthropology*
Their culture totemic,
they hear harps in can openers.
Art is a shredded couch, language
an even glare.

Best of all, to name a cat anything: Carbait, Rover,
Snot Rag, Exile, that kissing sound....

Slinky
(1992-2012)

Twenty years with this man—
grouting among hoarse words, moldy books,
and flat guitar strings—grown old as white oak.
The sleeping patterns of a kitten
and the coffee habit of a drunk
have aged him like droughted wood.
His women are like fleas,
one more like the long sting of a wasp, perhaps,
but now one with the soft burr
of a moonflower. He should set her to purring
in motion like a longboat across
the North Atlantic where his mind settles.

One day, he will sleep there.
One day, he will wake:
the ocean blue as metal,
his love as deep as graves.

God & Dog

The chain to my dog's throat
reminds him of eternity.
We are linked to our earthly forms
by mere vines of blood,
but in time we shall all be claimed
by one side of God or the other.

My dog and I shall stride
beneath the righteous hand of the Almighty,
while those southpawed, Satan-spawned wretches
eye-stabbing me from across the road
shall slip in a stream of their own spew
and slide screaming into a fire
tendered by generations of their meth-addled ilk.

My dog knows his master
and he will greet you with death.
He and I shall meet glory
and his chain shall guide him to the angels.

Dead Bird

Dead bird on the kitchen floor
You look half asleep
Cat can't wake you
Not even a peep
Hope you told your mother
That you're doing fine
So she won't come looking for you
Anytime...soon

Dead bird in the engine
Brought down the plane
You lost your future
But you won the game
Plane in the river
Looks like a duck
Looks like we're all running
Out of luck...soon

> *Black bird, blue bird*
> *Where did you go?*
> *Red bird, green bird*
> *Where's your home?*
> *Your nests in winter*
> *Look like graves*
> *When will you come back*
> *To save us...soon?*

Birds in the bushes
Flushed out by dogs
And bad men with rifles
Who mean you harm
Fat politicians
Who shoot their friends
They think their old world
Will never end...soon

Man dressed in feathers
Flew toward the sun
Fell in the ocean
Man, he was dumb
His story teaches
The limits of man
Dead bird you should listen
You'll understand…soon

Photo: Carly Cate

MARCK L. BEGGS earned his Ph.D. from the University of Denver, his M.F.A. from Warren Wilson College, and currently is a professor of English at Henderson State University in Arkansas. He is the author of four collections of poetry: *Blind Verse* (2015) *Catastrophic Chords* (2008), *Libido Café* (2004) and *Godworm* (1995). His poems have been published in numerous journals and magazines, including *Oxford American, Denver Quarterly, Poet Lore, Missouri Review, Exquisite Corpse, Toad Suck Review, Arkansas Review*, etc. In his spare time, he sings and plays guitar in the folk-rock band, *dog gods*. In 2009, he was selected by PETA as one of the top-10 vegetarians over the age of 50.